John O'William

Tales of Tillie

As Accompanied by John Williams

"If you read one feel-good book this year, you owe it to yourself to read *Tales of Tillie*. It is a wonderful book, which tells life tales from the point of view of Tillie, a kind and beautiful greyhound who was freed from the horrors of the race track. As Tillie's writing accompanist John Williams says, clearly Tillie adopted – and rescued – him!"

Ralph A. DeMeo, Chair Emeritus, The Florida Bar Animal Law Section

"My daughter was in an accident and spent six months in the hospital. As you can imagine, she felt very isolated and lonely, but when someone brought in a therapy dog to visit her, she was overwhelmed with joy. It was truly transformative for her. I hope everyone picks up a copy of *Tales of Tillie* so they can see a therapy dog in action and support TMH [Animal Therapy]."

Cheryl Hines, actress, producer and director best known for the award-winning series "Curb Your Enthusiasm"

Tales of Tillie

As Accompanied by John Williams

www.TalesOfTillie.com

Design donated by Harvest Print & Marketing Solutions, LLC
Tallahassee, Florida
harvest-press.com

ISBN-13: 9781736817506

First edition

Printed in the USA

Tales of Tillie

As Accompanied by John Williams

Dedicated to Tallahassee Memorial Animal Therapy and the 200 teams of animals and volunteers who bring joy, comfort, and peace to all they visit. A portion of the proceeds of this book supports their important work, so thank you for being a part of the family!

To learn more about the program, visit tmh.org/services/animal-therapy.

Preface by John Williams

There is a profound connection between animals and people that can be developed. There are numerous authors and articles about such, but the most powerful tool is to experience it. Tillie and I continue to have such an experience that began within the first moments of meeting until today some 10 years later.

Tillie walks with me pretty much every day at, around, or before sunrise on the shores of Lake Jackson. She protects, energizes, and calms me at the same time. We collectively produce a meaningful thought of some sort nearly every day that I can and do express as best I can in words. I usually take a picture to mark where we are and at what time when the thoughts occur. This book is a collection of some of that daily experience we enjoy.

Tillie knows we belong together. Tillie doesn't seem to think too much about ownership but rather about love and devotion, which she provides freely in large quantities. This book represents some of our moments together we are pleased to share.

Tillie is often referred to as a rescue. She raced at various tracks and won about half of her races for a couple of years using the name "Good Lookin." She is small for a greyhound, and it was apparently decided that she would be put to death—even though she ran extremely fast even for a greyhound. A local rescue group picked her up and Perry Henry picked her out and adopted her about 10 years ago. Perry had references to do so.

Tillie adopted me without references a little after Perry adopted her. Tillie apparently figured out what she wanted to know about me with no formal questionnaire. She has adopted a few others since and generally brings joy to everyone she meets. We hope *Tales of Tillie* brings everyone some joy and some insight.

Tillie's Introduction

People are interesting creatures. Even though I am not fluent in their human language, I understand emotional nuances. It seems that humans spend a lifetime being indoctrinated into the belief that, in the human experience, emotion is a sort of ugly stepchild that should only be acknowledged when there is a rational justification for it.

This axiom, that emotion is less valuable than reason and logic, seems to have been the unfortunate source of much violence against the human spirit. Perhaps because we non-humans have been spared this indoctrination, there is a certain wisdom and love that has been free to develop in us. Perhaps because we have not been saddled with the belief that certain aspects of the human experience are less worthy, we are able to provide comfort and understanding to humans that they find difficult to find elsewhere.

When I connect with humans, I notice that we both grow and heal into a wholeness beyond what the intellect alone can contemplate. Some might call that animal therapy. I leave that for you to decide.

GRATITUDES

I express my gratitude to Tillie for adopting me and for the kindness, loyalty, and wisdom she displays daily.

I express my gratitude to Perry Henry for allowing Tillie to adopt me and for being with us on our morning adventures.

I express my gratitude to Maureen O'Doogan for 25 years of collaboration about and study of the human condition which provides much of the basis for Tillie's thoughts about each day.

I express my gratitude to Anne Pettengill Munson who transformed an idea into a reality.

To you, the reader, I thank you for taking this journey with Tillie and me.

I thought it was a good morning for a walk.

Tillie told me every morning is a good morning for a walk.

Tillie said she likes looking at a new day with fresh eyes.

Tillie and I made it right at sunrise.

Tillie thinks timing can be important.

I told Tillie I enjoyed looking for beauty in all things.

Tillie told me I didn't have to look very hard as long as I was aware beauty existed everywhere.

I told Tillie I liked the tree. Tillie said let's climb it. I said maybe tomorrow. Tillie said I am concerned about your spirit of adventure.

Tillie said she enjoys the beauty of a cloudy morning.

I told Tillie sunrise this morning is spectacular.

Tillie said I am pleased you noticed.

I told Tillie watching the sun rise gives me hope for a good day.

Tillie said knowing my feelings well enough to express them seems time well spent.

I asked Tillie why she thought we get along so well.

She told me it is because she listens to me instead of giving me advice and that I am smart enough to give her treats every day.

Tillie started our walk without me this morning. We met at the lake. I told her she should be more obedient. I am not sure I could read her reaction.

I asked Tillie what she was doing near the puddles.

Tillie said she was reflecting.

Tillie thought it is a bit ominous looking this morning. I told her about weather alerts. Tillie told me that technology is cool but to keep my eyes open and pay attention to my intuition.

I asked Tillie if Gray could be the new Blue.

Tillie said it is generally a matter of perspective.

This morning's sky is similar to yesterday's but Tillie says different to the observant. She says I am hard to train but she will keep trying.

Tillie enjoys our walks. Sometimes she likes a leash sometimes not.

She advised me to go with the flow.

I asked Tillie if Friday mornings were better than other mornings.

Tillie said if you don't have to work Saturday they probably are.

Tillie told me every day is good but some are much better than others.

I told Tillie it seemed a little gloomy in the fog this morning.

Tillie said it was fine with her and gave her something else to experience.

Part of our path is grown over. Tillie made me go through first.

She said it was the gentlemanly thing to do.

I told Tillie there wasn't much to see this morning.

Tillie said look more carefully.

I told Tillie it seemed pretty muddy.

Tillie said yes it is. Let's have fun in the mud.

I told Tillie the week has been a little rough.

Tillie said it seems beautiful now.

Felt so good recently I started to jog while Tillie and I were walking.

It came back immediately to me that I intensely dislike jogging.

Tillie said it is good I am beginning to know myself.

Tillie said she loves the sunrise especially when she takes the time to appreciate it.

Tillie thinks every day is interesting.

I told Tillie that it seems like Monday.

Tillie said it happens fairly regularly this time of the week.

26

I told Tillie that she seems to find interesting smells everywhere.

She told me I could also with some patient practice.

I told Tillie that this seemed like another gray day. Tillie said it's Friday let's celebrate. I said Tillie you would probably say the same thing on Thursday. Tillie smiled.

28

Tillie thinks there is always light shining even through a stormy sky.

I told Tillie I wasn't certain about anything anymore.

Tillie told me good maybe I would be able to learn.

I told Tillie I appreciated actually seeing the sun this morning.

Tillie said the sun was there for me every morning whether I appreciated it or not.

31

Tillie likes the idea of always looking up.

I told Tillie something she apparently did not like and she stuck her tongue out at me. She has a mind of her own. I do not know who raised her.

I told Tillie maybe we should wait until the weather got better.

Tillie said let's enjoy now and if the weather gets better we can go again.

I was not sure why the sun was hiding today.

Tillie said everyone and everything needs rest sometimes.

I told Tillie that it seemed pretty overcast today.

Tillie told me that it was even more important that I be vigilant and not miss the beauty around me.

I asked Tillie why she is always sniffing everything. Tillie told me as she becomes more aware of everything she encounters her life becomes increasingly more enriched. I don't argue with Tillie.

Tillie said it is best not to become angry or frightened in troubled times.

I said that is hard. Tillie said I know.

I asked Tillie what she was looking at.

Tillie said it is strange that you do not know.

I told Tillie it is about to be chilly which rhymes with Tillie.

Tillie responded that I am special. I am not sure whether that is good or bad.

Tillie was being camera shy this morning. She said something about a bad hair day. I hope she wasn't talking about me.

I told Tillie it looks like it might rain.

Tillie said well let's enjoy the rain if it does.

Tillie said playing in the mud is still a hoot.

I explained to Tillie I couldn't walk this morning because I had a 6:45 appointment. Tillie reminded me that I could walk her but rather I chose something more important. She wasn't happy.

I asked Tillie if the hat made me look taller. She just snickered.

I explained to Tillie it was 34 degrees and I did not want to walk in the cold. We discussed it. Tillie's logic prevailed. I wish I could remember it. I would use it.

Tillie said sometimes there are no words.

The sky was beautiful this morning. Tillie voted for the weather not to get colder. I explained that she could not vote about weather. Tillie said that is discrimination. I never win an argument with her.

I asked Tillie if she celebrates Valentine's Day.

She said she has love in her heart for everyone but admits a bit more love for those who give her treats.

Tillie seemed interested in this tree.

She thinks curiosity keeps her young and vital.

I told Tillie the sun seemed friendly this morning.

Tillie said that is a good thing to be.

I told Tillie the sunrise was pretty.

Tillie said it was pretty close to perfect.

Tillie thinks Saturday is sniffulicious. I told her sniffulicious was hard to spell. Tillie said sometimes I miss the point.

I told Tillie she shouldn't run off without me.

Tillie said that criticism is mostly boring.

54

I told Tillie I would like to call every sunny day Sunday.

Tillie said fortunately or not I am not surprised.

I told Tillie it didn't seem like a very good day for a picture.

Tillie said if I look at it differently it might be.

I told Tillie I liked celebrating Friday.

Tillie said celebration is important.

I told Tillie I wasn't sure whether I was still sick or whether I was healing.

Tillie said that it depended on my point of view and level of self care.

Tillie says this picture shows that the sun *goes out of its way* to shine on all of us.

I asked Tillie what she was doing.

Tillie told me she enjoyed learning more about what was around her.

I told Tillie I like these but I didn't know what to call them.

Tillie said call them flowers.

Tillie thinks the sunrise on Sundays is a little more peaceful than other days.

I don't argue with her.

I told Tillie I was going to call our talks "Tales of Tillie."

She said alliteration is clever but inspiration is more important.

I love Tillie.

Tallahassee Memorial HealthCare Animal Therapy and How You Can Help

If you enjoyed *Tales of Tillie*, you understand how an animal can speak to you with comfort, patience, humor, and a certain wisdom that helps you deal with challenging experiences.

At Tallahassee Memorial HealthCare (TMH), over 200 therapy animals and their volunteers bring comfort to patients, families, and hospital staff. These special teams also visit nursing home and hospice patients, schools to encourage young readers, courthouses to comfort children testifying about horrifying situations, and first responders to give them a break from consistently stressful circumstances.

As a nonprofit, TMH Animal Therapy relies on volunteers and donors for the care and training of our "dogtors" and other animals. Generous donors also help us acquire "career change dogs" to serve in the most stressful of environments. Highly trained as service dogs (such as leader dogs for the blind), these exceptional dogs often did not graduate because they were too social to serve just one person. That makes the dog perfect for Animal Therapy!

Would you like to help comfort those in need through the special love of a therapy animal? When you donate to the TMH Foundation, you take part in their important work.

Special thanks to Krista Kleman and Harvest Print & Marketing Solutions, LLC for donating the design of this book.
Visit harvest-press.com to learn more.

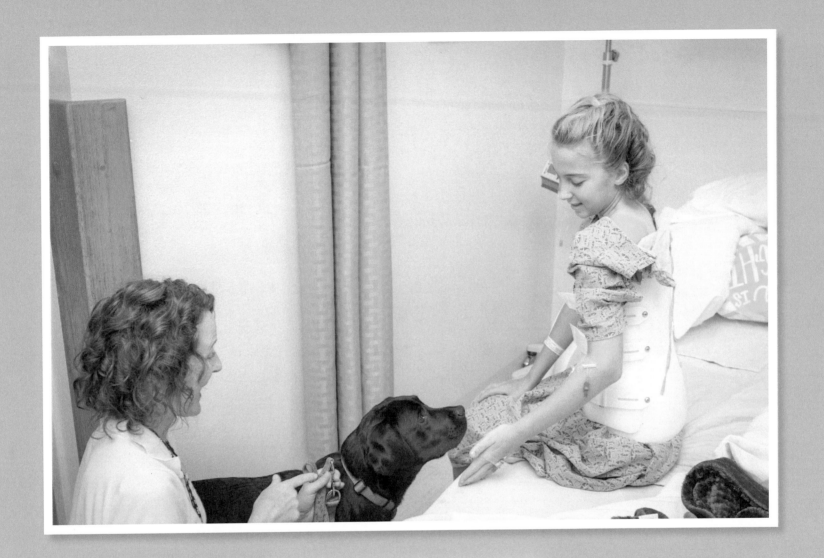

Visit tmhfoundation.org
and designate your gift to
Animal Therapy today.

Epilogue: "For Me?!?"

On April 5, 2021, in recognition of the therapy she provides every day, and in anticipation of the wisdom and comfort she will share with readers of *Tales of Tillie*, Tallahassee Memorial Animal Therapy surprised Tillie by making her an honorary member of the team.

Follow Tillie's future adventures at www.TalesOfTillie.com.

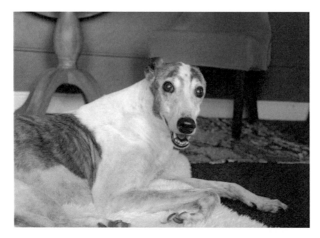

Scan the QR code to see Tillie receive her TMH bandana!

I asked Tillie how it felt to be honored. Tillie said honoring each other can be therapeutic and healing.

66

CPSIA information can be obtained
at www.ICGtesting.com
Printed in the USA
LVRC102245171221
706533LV00004B/39

* 9 7 8 1 7 3 6 8 1 7 5 0 6 *